BIOLOGY BASICS Need to Know

SilverTip

Photosynthesis

by Ruth Owen
Consultant: Jordan Stoleru
Science Educator

BEARPORT
PUBLISHING

Minneapolis, Minnesota

Credits

Cover and title page, © lovelyday12/Adobe Stock; 4–5, © Fahroni/Shutterstock; 6–7, © Vaclav Volrab/Shutterstock; 8, © Douglas Sacha/Shutterstock; 9, © 7activestudio/iStock; 11, © Radu Bercan/Shutterstock; 13, © PATTARAWIT CHOMPIPAT/Alamy; 14–15, © ArTDi101/Shutterstock; 16, © Chokniti-Studio/Shutterstock; 17, © AustralianCamera/Shutterstock; 19, © Vietnam Stock Images/Shutterstock; 21, © Stone36/Shutterstock; 23, © Lukas Kovarik/Shutterstock; 25, © 24K-Production/Shutterstock; 27, © Panupong Piewkleng/iStock; and 28, © Iftikhar Alam/Shutterstock.

Bearport Publishing Company Product Development Team

President: Jen Jenson; Director of Product Development: Spencer Brinker; Managing Editor: Allison Juda; Associate Editor: Naomi Reich; Associate Editor: Tiana Tran; Senior Designer: Colin O'Dea; Associate Designer: Elena Klinkner; Associate Designer: Kayla Eggert; Product Development Specialist: Anita Stasson

Library of Congress Cataloging-in-Publication Data is available at www.loc.gov or upon request from the publisher.

ISBN: 979-8-88822-037-5 (hardcover)
ISBN: 979-8-88822-229-4 (paperback)
ISBN: 979-8-88822-352-9 (ebook)

Copyright © 2024 Bearport Publishing Company. All rights reserved. No part of this publication may be reproduced in whole or in part, stored in any retrieval system, or transmitted in any form or by any means, electronic, mechanical, photocopying, recording, or otherwise, without written permission from the publisher.

For more information, write to Bearport Publishing, 5357 Penn Avenue South, Minneapolis, MN 55419.

Contents

Food for Life 4
Wonderful Water. 8
Turning Up the Gas 10
Cooking with Sunshine. 12
Breathable Bonus. 16
What's That Food For? 18
Out and In. 22
Energy for All 26

Photosynthesis in Action 28
SilverTips for Success 29
Glossary 30
Read More 31
Learn More Online 31
Index 32
About the Author 32

Food for Life

A tall tree reaches toward the sky. Every year, it grows new roots, branches, and leaves. How does the giant plant get all the energy it needs to do this? It makes its own food through photosynthesis (foh-toh-SIN-thi-sis).

From tall trees to tiny daisies, photosynthesis helps plants make food. Almost all plants get their energy this way. So do a few plantlike animals.

The food that plants need to live and grow is a sugar called **glucose** (GLOO-kose). It is made mostly in the tiny cells of a plant's leaves. To make this food, the plant must have three things. It needs water, a gas called **carbon dioxide**, and sunlight for photosynthesis.

Carbon dioxide is found in the air. People and animals breathe the gas out. Cars, trucks, and planes also make it. They pump out carbon dioxide when they burn fuels to move.

Wonderful Water

Most plants get the water they need from the soil around them. Their roots act a bit like straws to suck up the water. Then, plants send the water up their stems through thin tubes. Finally, the water moves into the leaves.

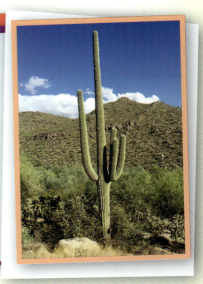

Cacti are desert plants. There isn't much water found in the dry soil nearby. So, these plants store water in their stems. That way, they have it when they need it.

Turning Up the Gas

The leaves are also where plants take in carbon dioxide. The gas comes in through tiny holes called **stomata** (STOH-muh-tuh). This happens mostly during the day.

At night, the stomata usually close up. Plants don't need carbon dioxide then. They can't do photosynthesis in the dark.

Stomata are found mostly on the undersides of leaves. They are too small for a person to see. Plants can have thousands of them.

Cooking with Sunshine

The last thing plants need to make food is sunlight. This is a form of energy from the sun. Plants make **chlorophyll** (KLOR-uh-fil) to take in the light. Chlorophyll also gives plants their green color. It is mostly in the leaves.

> In the fall, some green tree leaves turn yellow, red, or brown. That's because many trees stop making chlorophyll for the winter. They rest during these days with less light. Trees start doing photosynthesis again in the spring.

Chlorophyll inside a Leaf

With all the ingredients ready, it's time to get cooking. Plant leaves become little factories. They use the energy from the sun to break water and carbon dioxide into smaller parts. Then, the plant puts them back together in the form of glucose. It's time to eat!

Plants have xylem (ZYE-luhm) to carry water. These tubes travel from the roots to the leaves. Phloem (FLOH-em) goes the other way. Its tubes bring glucose throughout the plant.

Breathable Bonus

In addition to glucose, plants make **oxygen** during photosynthesis. But plants don't use this gas. For them, it is a **by-product**. Oxygen is let out through the same stomata that take in carbon dioxide.

All the oxygen in the air comes from plants and plantlike creatures. One of the biggest sources is in the ocean. Tiny, plantlike algae make a lot of oxygen.

Rain forests make a lot of oxygen on land.

What's That Food For?

After photosynthesis, what does a plant do with all that glucose? It uses some to keep itself healthy. Energy from the sugar can also help the plant grow bigger. Using glucose, a plant can make a new leaf, flower, fruit, or seed.

A plant also uses glucose to make **cellulose** (SEL-yuh-lohs). This forms the walls of plant cells. Plant stems have lots of tough cellulose. It keeps the plant standing straight and strong.

Fruits have seeds that can grow into more plants.

Sometimes, glucose is used to make energy in another way. Plants can go through **respiration** (res-puh-RAY-shuhn). This is a little like the opposite of photosynthesis. It does not need light.

During respiration, plants use glucose and take in oxygen. They make energy. The by-products are carbon dioxide and water.

Respiration can happen both during the day and at night. While it doesn't need light, light does not stop respiration from happening.

Out and In

Photosynthesis doesn't help only plants. Humans and other animals need oxygen to live.

The whole process helps keep life on Earth balanced. Plants release oxygen. Animals breathe it in. The moving creatures breathe out carbon dioxide. The plants take in the carbon dioxide. And so it goes on.

> About 21 percent of the air around Earth is oxygen. Less than 1 percent of air is carbon dioxide.

Although we breathe it out, carbon dioxide is harmful for us to take in. Too much of the gas in the air can also trap extra heat around the planet. This hurts Earth. By taking in carbon dioxide, plants keep animals safe and the planet cooler.

> Some heat from the sun bounces off Earth. It goes back into space. However, too much carbon dioxide acts like a blanket. It stops heat from leaving. This makes Earth hotter. It causes **climate change**.

Energy for All

Plants give us life. They take in energy from the sun to make their food. When humans and other animals eat those plants, they get the plants' energy. Anything that eats those plant-eaters gets energy, too. From oxygen to energy, we owe a lot to photosynthesis.

> Plants are important to most food webs. However, there wouldn't be any plants to eat without one thing. The sun gives us all life.

Photosynthesis in Action

Many things happen during photosynthesis to help plants make food.

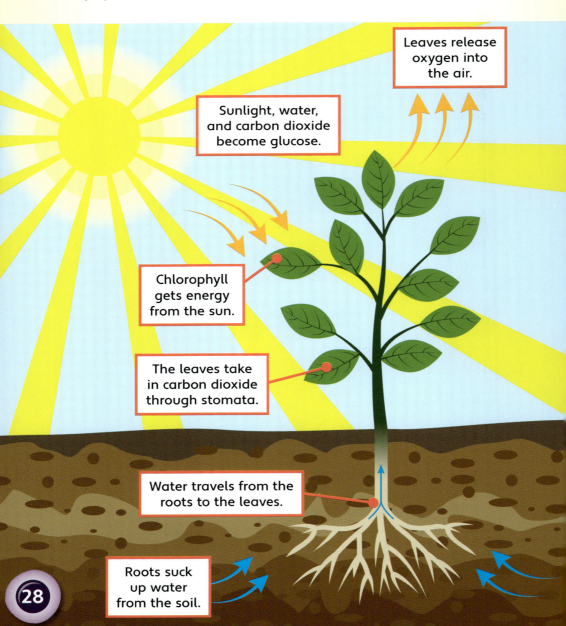

SilverTips for SUCCESS

★ SilverTips for REVIEW

Review what you've learned. Use the text to help you.

Define key terms

carbon dioxide   glucose
chlorophyll   oxygen
energy

Check for understanding

Name the three things that are needed for photosynthesis to happen.

What two things are made during photosynthesis?

How does a plant use the glucose it makes?

Think deeper

How would all life on Earth change if there were fewer plants?

★ SilverTips on TEST-TAKING

- **Make a study plan.** Ask your teacher what the test is going to cover. Then, set aside time to study a little bit every day.

- **Read all the questions carefully.** Be sure you know what is being asked.

- **Skip any questions** you don't know how to answer right away. Mark them and come back later if you have time.

Glossary

by-product something made in addition to the main object

carbon dioxide a gas necessary for the process of photosynthesis that is let out by animals as they breathe

cellulose parts of plants that mostly form cell walls

chlorophyll a substance in plants that traps sunlight

climate change changes in the usual weather around Earth, including the warming of the air and oceans, due to human activities

energy the power needed by all living things to grow and stay alive

glucose a sugar made by plants during photosynthesis

oxygen a gas plants make during photosynthesis that animals need to breathe

respiration the process by which plants take in oxygen and make energy

stomata tiny holes on a plant used for taking in carbon dioxide and letting out oxygen

Read More

Bolte, Mari. *How Plants Will Save the World (STEM to the Rescue).* Fremont, CA: Full Tilt Press, 2023.

Duling, Kaitlyn. *The Sun and Plants (The Power of the Sun).* New York: Cavendish Square, 2020.

London, Martha. *Photosynthesis (Discover Biology).* Minneapolis: ABDO Publishing, 2021.

Learn More Online

1. Go to **www.factsurfer.com** or scan the QR code below.

2. Enter "**Photosynthesis**" into the search box.

3. Click on the cover of this book to see a list of websites.

Index

by-product 16, 20

carbon dioxide 6–7, 10, 14, 16, 20, 22, 24, 28

chlorophyll 12–13, 28

energy 4, 12, 14, 18, 20, 26, 28

glucose 6, 14, 16, 18, 20, 28

leaves 4, 6, 8, 10–14, 18, 28

oxygen 16–17, 20, 22, 26, 28

respiration 20

roots 4, 8, 14, 28

soil 8, 28

stems 8, 18

stomata 10–11, 16, 28

sugar 6, 18

sunlight 6, 12, 14, 24, 26, 28

water 6, 8, 14, 20, 28

About the Author

Ruth Owen has been making books for more than 12 years. She lives in Cornwall, England, just minutes from the ocean. Ruth loves science so she likes to write books about plants and nature.